J. I. PACKER

*Five Studies for
Individuals or Groups*

KNOWING

GOD

BIBLE STUDY

*Fiftieth
Anniversary
Edition*

With DALE LARSEN *and* SANDY LARSEN

An imprint of InterVarsity Press
Downers Grove, Illinois

InterVarsity Press
P.O. Box 1400 | Downers Grove, IL 60515-1426
ivpress.com | email@ivpress.com

This study guide is adapted from J. I. Packer, *Meeting God*, LifeGuide® Bible Studies, ©1986 by InterVarsity Christian Fellowship of the United States of America, second edition ©2001 by J. I. Packer.

"Do We Desire to Know God?" is adapted from J. I. Packer, *Knowing God*, Americanized ed. (Downers Grove, IL: InterVarsity Press, 1993; first edition published 1973 by Hodder and Stoughton Limited, London).

InterVarsity Press® is the publishing division of InterVarsity Christian Fellowship/USA®. For more information, visit intervarsity.org.

All Scripture quotations, unless otherwise indicated, are taken from the *Holy Bible, New International Version®. NIV®.* Copyright ©1973, 1978, 1984 by International Bible Society. Used by permission of Zondervan Publishing House. All rights reserved.

While any stories in this book are true, some names and identifying information may have been changed to protect the privacy of individuals.

The publisher cannot verify the accuracy or functionality of website URLs used in this book beyond the date of publication.

Cover design: David Fassett

Interior design: Daniel van Loon

Cover images: Getty Images: © Peter Zelei Images, © Jackyenjoyphotography, © MirageC, © sergio34, © YOTUYA, © ulimi

ISBN 978-1-5140-0781-5 (print) | ISBN 978-1-5140-0855-3 (digital)

Printed in the United States of America ∞

CONTENTS

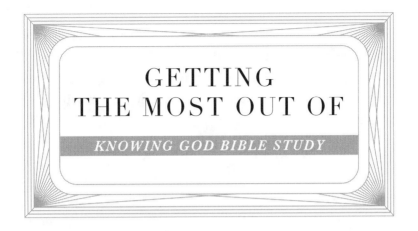

GETTING
THE MOST OUT OF
KNOWING GOD BIBLE STUDY

KNOWING CHRIST is where faith begins. From there we are shaped through the essentials of discipleship: Bible study, prayer, Christian community, worship, and much more. We learn to grow in Christlike character, pursue justice, and share our faith with others. We persevere through doubts and gain wisdom for daily life. Working through this series will help you practice the essentials by exploring biblical truths found in classic books.

HOW IT'S PUT TOGETHER

Each session includes a suggested reading from the book *Knowing God*, a session goal to help guide your study, reflection questions to stir your thoughts on the topic, the text of the Bible passage, questions for exploring the passage, response questions to help you apply what you've learned, and a closing suggestion for prayer.

The workbook format is ideal for personal study and also allows group members to prepare in advance for discussions and record discussion notes. The responses you write here can form a permanent record of your thoughts and spiritual progress.

Throughout the guide are study-note sidebars that may be useful for group leaders or individuals. These notes do not give the answers, but they do provide additional background information on certain questions and can challenge participants to think deeper or differently about the content.

WHAT KIND OF GUIDE IS THIS?

The studies are not designed to merely tell you what one person thinks. Instead, through inductive study, they will help you discover for yourself what Scripture is saying. Each study deals with a particular passage—rather than jumping around the Bible—so that you can really delve into the biblical author's meaning in that context.

The studies ask three different kinds of questions about the Bible passage:

* *Observation* questions help you to understand the content of the passage by asking about the basic facts: who, what, when, where, and how.

* *Interpretation* questions delve into the meaning of the passage.

* *Application* questions help you discover implications for growing in Christ in your own life.

These three keys unlock the treasures of the biblical writings and help you live them out.

This is a thought-provoking guide. Each question assumes a variety of answers. Many questions do not have "right" answers, particularly questions that aim at meaning or application. Instead, the questions should inspire readers to explore the passage more thoroughly.

This study guide is flexible. You can use it for individual study, but it is also great for a variety of groups—student, professional, neighborhood, or church groups. Each study takes about forty-five minutes in a group setting or thirty minutes in personal study.

SUGGESTIONS FOR INDIVIDUAL STUDY

1. This guide is a companion to a classic book that will enrich your spiritual life. If you have not read *Knowing God*, you may want to read the portion recommended in the "Read" section before you begin your study. The ideas in the book will enhance your study, but the Bible text will be the focus of each session.

2. Begin each session with prayer, asking God to speak to you from his Word about this particular topic.

3. As you read the Scripture passage, reproduced for you from the New International Version, you may wish to mark phrases that seem important. Note in the margin any questions that come to your mind.

4. Close with the suggested prayer. Speak to God about insights you have gained. Tell him of any desires you have for specific growth. Ask him to help you as you attempt to live out the principles described in that passage. You may wish to write your own prayer in this guide or a journal.

SUGGESTIONS FOR GROUP MEMBERS

Joining a Bible study group can be a great avenue to spiritual growth. Here are a few guidelines that will help you as you participate in the studies in this guide.

1. Reading the recommended portion of *Knowing God*, before or after each session, will enhance your study and understanding of the themes in this guide.

2. These studies use methods of inductive Bible study, which focuses on a particular passage of Scripture and works on it in depth. So try to dive into the given text instead of referring to other Scripture passages.

3. Questions are designed to help a group discuss together a passage of Scripture in order to understand its content, meaning, and implications. Most people are either natural talkers or natural listeners, yet this type of study works best if all members participate more or less evenly. Try to curb any natural tendency toward either excessive talking or excessive quiet. You and the rest of the group will benefit!

4. Most questions in this guide allow for a variety of answers. If you disagree with someone else's comment, gently say so. Then explain your own point of view from the passage before you.

5. Be willing to lead a discussion, if asked. Much of the preparation for leading has already been accomplished in the writing of this guide.

6. Respect the privacy of people in your group. Many people share things within the context of a Bible study group that they do not want to be public knowledge. Assume that personal information spoken within the group setting is private, unless you are specifically told otherwise.

7. We recommend that all groups agree on a few basic guidelines. You may wish to adapt this list to your situation:

    a. Anything said in this group is considered confidential and will not be discussed outside the group unless specific permission is given to do so.

    b. We will provide time for each person present to talk if he or she feels comfortable doing so.

   c. We will talk about ourselves and our own situations, avoiding conversation about other people.

   d. We will listen attentively to each other.

   e. We will pray for each other.

8. Enjoy your study. Prepare to grow!

SUGGESTIONS FOR GROUP LEADERS

There are specific suggestions to help you in the "Leading a Small Group" section. It describes how to lead a group discussion, gives helpful tips on group dynamics, and suggests ways to deal with problems that may arise during the discussion. With such helps, someone with little or no experience can lead an effective group study. Read this section carefully, even if you are leading only one group meeting.

INTRODUCTION

LOOKING FOR GOD

SINCE JESUS CHRIST CAPTURED ME many years ago, I have been what is called an *evangelical Christian*. As I move in evangelical circles, I am often troubled to find that while my fellow believers seek to advance in godliness, they show little direct interest in God himself. When they study Scripture, only the principles of daily personal godliness get their attention; their heavenly Father does not.

There is something narcissistic and even nutty in being more concerned about godliness than about God. As it would not be healthy to care more for our marriage than for the partner we have promised to love, honor, and cherish, so it is not healthy to care more for our religion than for the God whom we are called to daily praise and please.

While no single study guide can offer a comprehensive view of God, these studies are meant to provide an overview to encourage us to look for God every time we read the Bible. When I approach any biblical passage, I find it best to ask first what it shows me about God, second what it shows me about human life here and hereafter, and only then, as my third question, what it says to me about my life today.

Though these studies are inductive in form, they take for granted some overarching biblical perspectives.

First, we know about God through his own self-revelation in the Bible. All human ideas, both traditional and contemporary, about God's will, works, and ways must be ruthlessly brought into line with what Scripture says. Idolatry—forming unbiblical notions of God, and so worshiping unrealities—is the sin that Scripture denounces most frequently.

Second, we know God definitively through our Lord Jesus Christ, who is God incarnate. The one who sees Jesus sees the Father fully reflected (see John 14:9). As God incarnate, Jesus is God for man and man for God. As our Prophet, Priest, and King (Teacher, Savior, Lord), he brings God's eternal truth, pardoning mercy, and royal protection to us. And as the One who was crucified, raised, and enthroned for us, he brings us to God (see 1 Peter 3:18). He is the eternal Son through whom the Father created and sustains his world (Colossians 1:15-17). He is, and always was, the One through whom all life (conscious existence) and all light (knowledge of reality) are given to the human race (John 1:4). All God's mercy and truth were mediated through him from the beginning—even before his incarnation. It is right to see him in all Old Testament passages that present God's revelation and grace.

Third, the true God whom Christians know is tripersonal: Father, Son, and Holy Spirit. Three coequal, coeternal persons exist within the unity of one God, who is thus both *he* and *they*. As with all other aspects of the mystery of God, we know from Scripture that this is true, though it is beyond us to conceive how it can be so. Scripture tells us that the three who are one function as a perfect team in the divine works of creation, providence, and salvation.

Redemption was arranged by the Father, was accomplished by the Son, and is applied by the Spirit, whom the Father and the Son together sent into the world for that purpose. The Father wills that we honor the Son; the Son wills that we honor the Father; the Spirit works to bring us to the place where in faith, love, and prayerful obedience we honor the Father and Son and celebrate in worship the grace and power that flow to us from all three. This God-centered, Christ-centered, Spirit-centered, Trinity-centered perspective is constant in the New Testament. All that is said of God in the Old Testament should be set within this frame. The Lord God, the Holy One of Israel, always was Father, Son, and Holy Spirit, although this triunity was not revealed until the Son became flesh.

Fourth, when all is said and done, our Creator is bound to surpass our comprehension. Though our knowledge of him may be true as far as it goes, it will necessarily be incomplete. It is difficult to avoid well-intentioned error and one-sidedness when thinking of God. As a reference point for balance and breadth, the resources section of this book suggests several works that clearly present the Christian view of God.

It is my prayer that by studying these Scripture passages you will gain a deeper knowledge of the God we worship and serve.

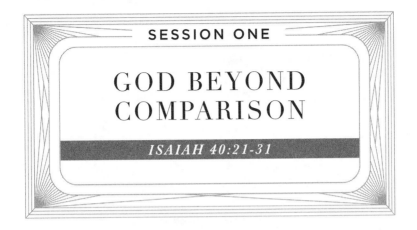

ADVERTISERS TRY TO PERSUADE US that their product is superior to all competition. In the most superlative language they tell us that what they offer is bigger, speedier, more powerful, more efficient, and in every sense better than anything else on the market. Much of the time we don't believe these claims of superiority since every product claims to be better than every other. But what if we came across something so great it couldn't be compared to anything? Is there anything or anyone beyond comparison?

SESSION GOAL	READ
Enlarge our thoughts about God and learn to wait on him for strength.	Chapters one through four of *Knowing God*

 REFLECT

* What have you heard God compared to?

✳ Have you experienced problems you feared God was not big
enough to handle or might not care about? What were they
(or what are they)?

 STUDY

READ ISAIAH 40:21-31

In this passage the prophet Isaiah makes statements about God;
yet there is an overwhelming sensation that God himself is
speaking here about himself. In fact, in some places God does
speak in the first person.

²¹Do you not know?
   Have you not heard?
Has it not been told you from the beginning?
   Have you not understood since the earth was founded?
²²He sits enthroned above the circle of the earth,
   and its people are like grasshoppers.
He stretches out the heavens like a canopy,
   and spreads them out like a tent to live in.
²³He brings princes to naught
   and reduces the rulers of this world to nothing.
²⁴No sooner are they planted,
   no sooner are they sown,
   no sooner do they take root in the ground,
than he blows on them and they wither,
   and a whirlwind sweeps them away like chaff.

²⁵"To whom will you compare me?
   Or who is my equal?" says the Holy One.

²⁶Lift up your eyes and look to the heavens:
Who created all these?
He who brings out the starry host one by one
and calls forth each of them by name.
Because of his great power and mighty strength,
not one of them is missing.

²⁷Why do you complain, Jacob?
Why do you say, Israel,
"My way is hidden from the LORD;
my cause is disregarded by my God"?
²⁸Do you not know?
Have you not heard?
The LORD is the everlasting God,
the Creator of the ends of the earth.
He will not grow tired or weary,
and his understanding no one can fathom.
²⁹He gives strength to the weary
and increases the power of the weak.
³⁰Even youths grow tired and weary,
and young men stumble and fall;
³¹but those who hope in the LORD
will renew their strength.
They will soar on wings like eagles;
they will run and not grow weary,
they will walk and not be faint.

1. What characteristics of the Lord do you find in this passage?

2. What does God remind the people of in verses 21-22?

3. Why does God challenge people to compare him to anyone or anything else (vv. 23-26)?

At various times in Israel's history, the false gods of other nations drew them away from the true God. Israel also made political alliances to try to guarantee their safety rather than relying on the Lord. Perhaps God was reminding them through Isaiah that human help is ultimately futile, at least when it tries to oppose him or get around his purposes.

4. Israel complained that God seemed distant and uncaring (v. 27). How does this entire passage answer that charge?

5. How are we often like Israel in our complaints?

At the time Isaiah wrote, in the seventh century BC, the apathetic nation of Israel was devoid of hope and vitality because they thought their God had lost interest in them and left them to sink. Isaiah presents God as eternal and infinite, sovereign and gracious, ready to renew the strength of all who look patiently and hopefully in his direction.

6. Consider the images of God's relation to the natural world. What effect do they make on the reader?

7. Given the fact that we have this incomparable God, why do you think people try to tell him how to run things, whether the world or their own lives?

This passage begins with the question "Do you not know?" Of course Israel could recite the facts about God's power, wisdom, and love, just as we can. But our real knowledge of God is only as great as our faith. Therefore, we need to be constantly reminded and challenged about our view of God.

8. What does God promise to those who feel weary and without strength (vv. 28-31)?

RESPOND

✳ In what areas of your life do you especially need to admit that God knows and understands more than you do?

✳ Consider aspects or times in your life in which you feel weary and powerless. How can the truths of this Scripture passage refresh and strengthen you?

PRAY

As you pray, express trust in the Lord. Thank him for loving you and sending his Son for you, no matter how weak or insignificant you may feel. Thank him for renewing you with his strength.

NEXT STEPS

This week, make a conscious effort to watch for evidence of the Creator in the natural world he has made. You can do this whether you live in an urban, suburban, or rural area. Make notes of what you notice and what your observations show you about God.

GOD'S UNFAILING FAITHFULNESS

PSALM 107:1-32

"**WE WERE OUT IN THE BOAT** and this storm came up suddenly and the waves got bigger and bigger . . ." "It was getting dark and cold, and I realized I was lost . . ." "I had made such a mess of things, I didn't know how I'd ever get out of the situation . . ." Stories like these grab our attention because we want to hear how they turn out. Psalm 107 is a series of dramatic "short stories" that make us keep asking, "What happened next?"

SESSION GOAL	**READ**
Be encouraged to trust God's delivering power in every situation of need.	Chapters five through nine of *Knowing God*

 **REFLECT**

❋ When you go out of your way to do something for someone, do you expect to be thanked? Why or why not?

❋ When have you been especially grateful for something someone did for you? How did you thank that person?

STUDY

READ PSALM 107:1-32

¹Give thanks to the LORD, for he is good;
  his love endures forever.

²Let the redeemed of the LORD tell their story—
  those he redeemed from the hand of the foe,
³those he gathered from the lands,
  from east and west, from north and south.

⁴Some wandered in desert wastelands,
  finding no way to a city where they could settle.
⁵They were hungry and thirsty,
  and their lives ebbed away.
⁶Then they cried out to the LORD in their trouble,
  and he delivered them from their distress.
⁷He led them by a straight way
  to a city where they could settle.
⁸Let them give thanks to the LORD for his unfailing love
  and his wonderful deeds for mankind,
⁹for he satisfies the thirsty
  and fills the hungry with good things.

¹⁰Some sat in darkness, in utter darkness,
  prisoners suffering in iron chains,

[11]because they rebelled against God's commands
and despised the plans of the Most High.
[12]So he subjected them to bitter labor;
they stumbled, and there was no one to help.
[13]Then they cried to the LORD in their trouble,
and he saved them from their distress.
[14]He brought them out of darkness, the utter darkness,
and broke away their chains.
[15]Let them give thanks to the LORD for his unfailing love
and his wonderful deeds for mankind,
[16]for he breaks down gates of bronze
and cuts through bars of iron.

[17]Some became fools through their rebellious ways
and suffered affliction because of their iniquities.
[18]They loathed all food
and drew near the gates of death.
[19]Then they cried to the LORD in their trouble,
and he saved them from their distress.
[20]He sent out his word and healed them;
he rescued them from the grave.
[21]Let them give thanks to the LORD for his unfailing love
and his wonderful deeds for mankind.
[22]Let them sacrifice thank offerings
and tell of his works with songs of joy.

[23]Some went out on the sea in ships;
they were merchants on the mighty waters.
[24]They saw the works of the LORD,
his wonderful deeds in the deep.
[25]For he spoke and stirred up a tempest
that lifted high the waves.

²⁶They mounted up to the heavens and went down to
    the depths;
  in their peril their courage melted away.
²⁷They reeled and staggered like drunkards;
  they were at their wits' end.
²⁸Then they cried out to the LORD in their trouble,
  and he brought them out of their distress.
²⁹He stilled the storm to a whisper;
  the waves of the sea were hushed.
³⁰They were glad when it grew calm,
  and he guided them to their desired haven.
³¹Let them give thanks to the LORD for his unfailing love
  and his wonderful deeds for mankind.
³²Let them exalt him in the assembly of the people
  and praise him in the council of the elders.

1. In verses 4-9, 10-16, 17-22, and 23-32, the psalmist relates
   four different incidents. What elements do all four stories
   have in common?

Possible titles for these four incidents are
"Desert Survivors" (vv. 4-9); "Rebellion Forgiven"
(vv. 10-16); "Sickness Healed" (vv. 17-22);
"Sailors Rescued" (vv. 23-32).

2. How is God's faithfulness demonstrated in each of the four accounts?

> It makes no difference whether trouble comes because we ask for it by sinning (vv. 11, 17) or simply because things go wrong (vv. 4-5, 24-27). Today, as in the time this psalm was written, the only issue is whether we cry out to God when in trouble, confessing our sin and need, putting our lives in his hands, and pleading for deliverance.

3. Each scene concludes by describing God's salvation and calling us to give thanks for his unfailing love (vv. 8, 15, 21-22, 31-32). Why is it good to thank God?

4. According to verses 22 and 32, what are some appropriate ways we can give thanks to God?

Regardless of the specific events referred to in this psalm, it is clearly meant to apply beyond Israel's situation to anyone who cries out to God and experiences his unfailing faithfulness. Thankful celebration of God's goodness and unfailing love in the past will fortify us to trust him when trouble arises, present or future.

5. What does this Scripture reveal about God's hand in the ups and downs of our lives?

6. Each scene begins by describing a calamity and a desperate cry for help. Why do you think we so often have to hit bottom before we cry out to God?

7. What specific things do you think God would want you to pay attention to in this psalm?

✳ RESPOND ✳

✳ With which of the four scenes in Psalm 107 do you identify most and why?

✳ What prayers has God answered recently for which you are thankful?

✳ PRAY ✳

Thank God for his past deliverances from trouble. Express both your trust in him and your need for his help in those situations where you are still in the middle of difficulty.

✳ NEXT STEPS ✳

Is there someone for whom you regret not showing enough gratitude? Write and send that person a letter expressing your thanks. Be specific about why you are grateful. You can write the letter even if you are unable to contact the person.

Write your own "Psalm 107," recalling times you cried out to the Lord in distress and he delivered you.

GOD: FATHER, SON, SPIRIT

JOHN 14:1-11; 16:5-15

OUR NORMAL DAYS ARE FILLED WITH a gnat-like cloud of details, most of them about as important as gnats. Take care of this, see to that. We talk about mundane things as life chugs along in its ordinary routine.

Then a crisis hits! Suddenly there's no luxury of time for inconsequential chatter. We forget insignificant details and talk about what's vital to us. That was the situation of Jesus and his disciples the night before Jesus was crucified. At their final meal together, they talked far into the night about the most important issues.

SESSION GOAL	READ
Honor and worship God as revealed in the three persons of the Trinity.	Chapters ten through thirteen of *Knowing God*

 REFLECT

✳ Complete this sentence: "I think God would be more real to me if . . ."

✳ Have you ever wished or even prayed that God would show himself to you? Why (or why not)?

STUDY

READ JOHN 14:1-11

John 13–17 records Jesus' words on the night he ate the Last Supper with his disciples.

¹"Do not let your hearts be troubled. You believe in God; believe also in me. ²My Father's house has many rooms; if that were not so, would I have told you that I am going there to prepare a place for you? ³And if I go and prepare a place for you, I will come back and take you to be with me that you also may be where I am. ⁴You know the way to the place where I am going."

⁵Thomas said to him, "Lord, we don't know where you are going, so how can we know the way?"

⁶Jesus answered, "I am the way and the truth and the life. No one comes to the Father except through me. ⁷If you really know me, you will know my Father as well. From now on, you do know him and have seen him."

⁸Philip said, "Lord, show us the Father and that will be enough for us."

⁹Jesus answered: "Don't you know me, Philip, even after I have been among you such a long time? Anyone who has seen me has seen the Father. How can you say, 'Show us the Father'? ¹⁰Don't you believe that I am in the Father,

and that the Father is in me? The words I say to you I do not speak on my own authority. Rather, it is the Father, living in me, who is doing his work. [11]Believe me when I say that I am in the Father and the Father is in me; or at least believe on the evidence of the works themselves."

1. The disciples must have felt confused and anxious when Jesus announced that he was going away (vv. 2-5). What reassurances did he offer them for the future?

2. How has Jesus changed the way that human beings can relate to God?

3. Reflect on Jesus' remarkable statements in verses 6-7. Why is he the only person who can truthfully make these claims about himself?

> Jesus is not simply one way to see the Father. He is the full and final revelation of the Father. There is no other way to see the Father clearly and directly than through Jesus. This is not only true for the disciples; it is and always will be true for us as well. This is one reason why there is no other way to the Father apart from Jesus.

4. After Jesus said that the disciples had seen the Father, Philip still asked to see the Father (vv. 7-8). What had Philip failed to grasp about the relationship of the Father and the Son (vv. 9-11)?

READ JOHN 16:5-15

⁵"But now I am going to him who sent me. None of you asks me, 'Where are you going?' ⁶Rather, you are filled with grief because I have said these things. ⁷But very truly I tell you, it is for your good that I am going away. Unless I go away, the Advocate will not come to you; but if I go, I will send him to you. ⁸When he comes, he will prove the world to be in the wrong about sin and righteousness and judgment: ⁹about sin, because people do not believe in me; ¹⁰about righteousness, because I am going to the Father, where you can see me no longer; ¹¹and about judgment, because the prince of this world now stands condemned.

¹²"I have much more to say to you, more than you can now bear. ¹³But when he, the Spirit of truth, comes, he will

guide you into all the truth. He will not speak on his own; he will speak only what he hears, and he will tell you what is yet to come. ¹⁴He will glorify me because it is from me that he will receive what he will make known to you. ¹⁵All that belongs to the Father is mine. That is why I said the Spirit will receive from me what he will make known to you."

5. What further assurances did Jesus offer his grieving disciples (vv. 5-7)?

6. The Holy Spirit proves the world wrong in regard to sin, righteousness, and judgment (vv. 8-11). In your own words, explain how the world is wrong about these things.

> It is important to realize that everything the Spirit does in this passage—testify, convict, guide into truth, and bring glory—all focuses on Jesus Christ. Just as the Spirit testifies about Jesus and glorifies him, we must follow the Spirit's example.

7. How does the Holy Spirit make Christ known to us?

8. How does this Scripture passage help you understand the Holy Spirit's unique ministry to you and to the world?

It is the combined testimony of the Spirit of Jesus and the disciples of Jesus that God uses to reach the world. If we assume that evangelism is the Holy Spirit's task and not ours, we avoid our responsibility. Likewise, if we assume we are sufficient by ourselves to reach others, we will lack the Holy Spirit's power.

RESPOND

✳ In what sense have you seen God the Father in and through Jesus Christ?

✳ How do you see yourself fitting in with the ministry of the Holy Spirit in the world?

PRAY

Thank God for the revelation that he is one: the Father, the Son, and the Holy Spirit in unity. Pray for a spirit of openness that you will be sensitive to God's guidance in your life as well as his reassurance of his love for you.

NEXT STEPS

Complete the picture by reading all of John 13–17. What additional light does the passage shed on this study?

DO WE DESIRE
TO KNOW GOD?

If we truly desire to know God, two things follow.

First, we must recognize how much we lack knowledge of God. We must learn to measure ourselves, not by our knowledge about God, not by our gifts and responsibilities in the church, but by how we pray and what goes on in our hearts. Many of us have no idea how impoverished we are at this level. Let us ask the Lord to show us.

Second, we must seek the Savior. When he was on earth, he invited ordinary people to company with him; thus they came to know him, and in knowing him to know his Father. The Old Testament records pre-incarnate manifestations of the Lord Jesus doing the same thing—companying with men and women, in character as the angel of the Lord, in order that they might know him. The Lord Jesus Christ is now absent from us in body, but spiritually it makes no difference; still we may find and know God through seeking and finding Jesus' company. It is those who have sought the Lord Jesus till they have found him—for the promise is that when we seek him with all our hearts, we shall surely find him—who can stand before the world to testify that they have known God.

GOD'S MERCIFUL DISCIPLINE

HEBREWS 12:1-13

YOU'RE RUNNING YOUR FIRST MARATHON, and after thirteen miles, you're about ready to quit. Another thirteen miles—no, 13.2!—to go. Your legs are aching, your chest is burning, and you can't remember why you even entered this race. How good it would be to stop, to lie down and rest, to take it easy. Then you think of your friends and family who are cheering you on. You think of your trainer who helped you prepare for this race. You remember how they have all encouraged you to keep going because it will all be worth it when you cross the finish line. And you keep running!

The Christians to whom the letter of Hebrews was written had the same thoughts about the Christian life. They were in danger of weakening in their faith. The writer of Hebrews encouraged them to keep running through the pain, because finishing the race would be worth all their struggle.

SESSION GOAL	**READ**
Understand and accept difficulties as part of God's loving discipline.	Chapters fourteen through seventeen of *Knowing God*

⚜ REFLECT ⚜

✳ When have you especially needed endurance, whether physical, emotional, mental, or spiritual?

✳ How has the faithfulness of other Christian believers motivated you to keep going?

⚜ STUDY ⚜

READ HEBREWS 12:1-13

[1]Therefore, since we are surrounded by such a great cloud of witnesses, let us throw off everything that hinders and the sin that so easily entangles. And let us run with perseverance the race marked out for us, [2]fixing our eyes on Jesus, the pioneer and perfecter of faith. For the joy set before him he endured the cross, scorning its shame, and sat down at the right hand of the throne of God. [3]Consider him who endured such opposition from sinners, so that you will not grow weary and lose heart.

[4]In your struggle against sin, you have not yet resisted to the point of shedding your blood. [5]And have you completely forgotten this word of encouragement that addresses you as a father addresses his son? It says,

"My son, do not make light of the Lord's discipline,
  and do not lose heart when he rebukes you,
⁶because the Lord disciplines the one he loves,
  and he chastens everyone he accepts as his son."

⁷Endure hardship as discipline; God is treating you as his children. For what children are not disciplined by their father? ⁸If you are not disciplined—and everyone undergoes discipline—then you are not legitimate, not true sons and daughters at all. ⁹Moreover, we have all had human fathers who disciplined us and we respected them for it. How much more should we submit to the Father of spirits and live! ¹⁰They disciplined us for a little while as they thought best; but God disciplines us for our good, in order that we may share in his holiness. ¹¹No discipline seems pleasant at the time, but painful. Later on, however, it produces a harvest of righteousness and peace for those who have been trained by it.

¹²Therefore, strengthen your feeble arms and weak knees. ¹³"Make level paths for your feet," so that the lame may not be disabled, but rather healed.

1. "Therefore" at the beginning of this passage refers to the roll of people of faith in Hebrews 11. They are the "great cloud of witnesses." What kind of life do they inspire us to live (vv. 1-3)?

In the dominant culture in which the original readers lived, runners in races shed everything that would hinder them, both excess weight and extra or loose-fitting garments. (In fact, the Greek custom was for runners to strip naked.) The writer pictures a stadium filled with people who have already run the race. The spectators are cheering on those who are still running for the finish line.

2. Believers are told to fix their eyes on Jesus as they run "the race marked out for us" (vv. 1-2). What are some practical ways to do this?

3. The metaphor changes at verse 5. What do athletic training and parental discipline have in common?

4. Why should God's discipline encourage us rather than dishearten us?

"God's sovereign hand is at work as much through life's adversities as in its joys and pleasures. He may well be saying something extremely important to us through our troubles that we could not or would not easily receive if everything went well for us at all times."*

5. If believers submit to the heavenly Father's discipline, how will their lives be different (vv. 10-13)?

6. What are some down-to-earth examples of "a harvest of righteousness and peace" (v. 11)?

7. In practical terms, how can believers strengthen themselves and make level paths for their feet (vv. 12-13)?

Worship, studying Scripture, obedience to God, talking about God with other believers, witnessing to nonbelievers, carrying personal reminders of his faithfulness—these are all ways to focus on Christ, strengthen ourselves, and move forward on a level path.

8. We would probably all prefer to go through life free of problems and difficulties. How does this passage contradict that idealized picture?

RESPOND

* What good fruits have you experienced from submitting to the Lord's discipline?

* In order to run your race with perseverance, what hindrances or entanglements do you need to cast off (v. 1)? What steps will you take to do this?

PRAY

Pray that you will recognize your Father's discipline when it comes, and that you will submit to it and let it bring about the changes he wants to make in you.

NEXT STEPS

How can you encourage someone else in their race this week?

---

*Raymond Brown, *The Message of Hebrews* (Downers Grove, IL: IVP Academic, 1982), 232.

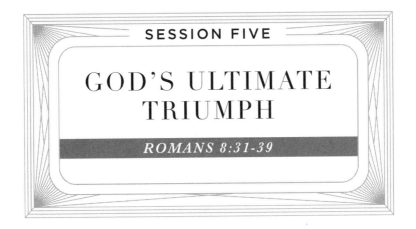

GOD'S ULTIMATE TRIUMPH

ROMANS 8:31-39

PICTURE A COURTROOM IN WHICH YOU STAND ACCUSED, and you know you are guilty. With a sick feeling of dread you await your sentence. Then your defense attorney steps forward and says, "I have already taken the punishment and paid the penalty for this person's crimes." In disbelief you look up at the judge, and the judge nods in agreement. All charges against you are dropped. Case dismissed. You have been declared innocent!

That is the dramatic picture Paul draws in this Scripture passage. God is the judge, and Christ is our defender. In the words of a prison chaplain we know, "Jesus is our defense attorney, and he's never lost a case!"

SESSION GOAL	READ
Gain unshakable assurance of God's forgiveness for sin and triumph over evil.	Chapters eighteen through twenty-two of *Knowing God*

 REFLECT

✳ What makes you feel like a conqueror?

✳ What makes you feel like the conquered?

STUDY

READ ROMANS 8:31-39

³¹What, then, shall we say in response to these things? If God is for us, who can be against us? ³²He who did not spare his own Son, but gave him up for us all—how will he not also, along with him, graciously give us all things? ³³Who will bring any charge against those whom God has chosen? It is God who justifies. ³⁴Who then is the one who condemns? No one. Christ Jesus who died—more than that, who was raised to life—is at the right hand of God and is also interceding for us. ³⁵Who shall separate us from the love of Christ? Shall trouble or hardship or persecution or famine or nakedness or danger or sword? ³⁶As it is written:

"For your sake we face death all day long;
    we are considered as sheep to be slaughtered."

³⁷No, in all these things we are more than conquerors through him who loved us. ³⁸For I am convinced that neither death nor life, neither angels nor demons, neither the present nor the future, nor any powers, ³⁹neither height nor depth, nor anything else in all creation, will be able to separate us from the love of God that is in Christ Jesus our Lord.

1. How would you describe the overall mood of this passage?

The phrase "these things" (v. 31) refers to all that leads up to this passage in Romans 8, including the ideas that Christ is the sufficient offering for our sin, the Holy Spirit lives in us and we should be governed by him, the Spirit gives us life, we are God's children, we have hope for the future, and we are called and justified by God.

2. Why can Christians be confident that God holds no accusations against us?

3. How does Paul describe the generosity of God (v. 32)?

4. Christ himself intercedes with God the Father for us (v. 34).
   How can that truth increase our confidence in God's love
   and care for us even more?

5. In spite of God's reassurances, how might the difficulties in
   verse 35 make Christians feel that they have been separated
   from the love of Christ?

Paul asks, "Who then is the one who condemns?" and
answers, "No one" (v. 34). Yet Satan, other people,
and even our own consciences may accuse us of
being guilty and unacceptable to God. Such charges
cannot hold up in the heavenly court because Christ
himself has died to pay for our sin. What's more, he
lives today and is interceding for us right now.

6. In the space of two sentences, Paul moves from the reality of
   vicious persecution to the statement that "we are more than
   conquerors" (vv. 36-37). How can both be true?

7. Paul calls us "*more* than conquerors." What do you think he means by this added intensifier?

RESPOND

✳ What victories have you experienced when you submitted difficult situations to the Lord?

✳ What are some areas of life where you want and need God to give you victory and make you a conqueror in his strength?

PRAY

Thank the Lord Jesus Christ for dying and rising for you, which qualifies him to be your defense attorney. Tell him about any ways that you feel guilty or unacceptable to God, and accept his mercy. Pray that rather than being one of the conquered, you will be a conqueror.

 NEXT STEPS

Read and study Romans 8:1-30. How does it lead up to today's passage?

LEADING A SMALL GROUP

LEADING A BIBLE DISCUSSION can be an enjoyable and rewarding experience. But it can also be intimidating—especially if you've never done it before. If this is how you feel, you're in good company.

Remember when God asked Moses to lead the Israelites out of Egypt? Moses replied, "Please send someone else" (Exodus 4:13)! But God gave Moses the help (human and divine) he needed to be a strong leader.

Leading a Bible discussion is not difficult if you follow certain guidelines. You don't need to be an expert on the Bible or a trained teacher. The suggestions listed below can help you to effectively fulfill your role as leader—and enjoy doing it.

PREPARING FOR THE STUDY

1. As you study the passage before the group meeting, ask God to help you understand it and apply it in your own life. Unless this happens, you will not be prepared to lead others. Pray too for the various members of the group. Ask God to open your hearts to the message of his Word and motivate you to action.

2. Read the introduction to the entire guide to get an overview of the subject at hand and the issues that will be explored.

3. Be ready to respond to the "Reflect" questions with a personal story or example. The group will be only as vulnerable and open as its leader.

4. Read the chapter of the companion book that is recommended at the beginning of the session.

5. Read and reread the assigned Bible passage to familiarize yourself with it. You may want to look up the passage in a Bible so that you can see its context.

6. This study guide is based on the New International Version of the Bible. It will help you and the group if you use this translation as the basis for your study and discussion.

7. Carefully work through each question in the study. Spend time in meditation and reflection as you consider how to respond.

8. Write your thoughts and responses in the space provided in the study guide. This will help you to express your understanding of the passage clearly.

9. It might help you to have a Bible dictionary handy. Use it to look up any unfamiliar words, names, or places.

10. Take the final (application) study questions and the "Respond" portion of each study seriously. Consider what this means for your life, what changes you may need to make in your lifestyle, or what actions you can take in your church or with people you know. Remember that the group will follow your lead in responding to the studies.

LEADING THE STUDY

1. Be sure everyone in your group has a study guide and a Bible. Encourage the group to prepare beforehand for each discussion by reading the introduction to the guide and by working through the questions for that session.

2. At the beginning of your first time together, explain that these studies are meant to be discussions, not lectures. Encourage the members of the group to participate. However, do not put pressure on those who may be hesitant to speak during the first few sessions.

3. Begin the study on time. Open with prayer, asking God to help the group understand and apply the passage.

4. Have a group member read aloud the introductory paragraph at the beginning of the discussion. This will remind the group of the topic of the study.

5. Discuss the "Reflect" questions before reading the Bible passage. These kinds of opening questions are important for several reasons. First, there is usually a stiffness that needs to be overcome before people will begin to talk openly. A good question will break the ice.

   Second, most people will have lots of different things going on in their minds (dinner, an exam, an important meeting coming up, how to get the car fixed) that have nothing to do with the study. A creative question will get their attention and draw them into the discussion.

   Third, opening questions can reveal where our thoughts or feelings need to be transformed by Scripture. That is why it is important not to read the passage before the "Reflect" questions are asked. The passage will tend to color the honest reactions people would otherwise give because they feel they are supposed to think the way the Bible does.

6. Have a group member read aloud the Scripture passage.

7. As you ask the questions, keep in mind that they are designed to be used just as they are written. You may simply read them aloud. Or you may prefer to express them in your own words.

   There may be times when it is appropriate to deviate from the study guide. For example, a question may already have been answered. If so, move on to the next question. Or someone may raise an important question not covered in the guide. Take time to discuss it, but try to keep the group from going off on tangents.

8. Avoid offering the first answer to a study question. Repeat or rephrase questions if necessary until they are clearly understood. An eager group quickly becomes passive and silent if members think the leader will give all the *right* answers.

9. Don't be afraid of silence. People may need time to think about the question before formulating their answers.

10. Don't be content with just one answer. Ask, "What do the rest of you think?" or, "Anything else?" until several people have given answers to a question. You might point out one of the study sidebars to help spur discussion; for example, "Does the quotation on page seventeen provide any insight as you think about this question?"

11. Acknowledge all contributions. Be affirming whenever possible. Never reject an answer. If it is clearly off base, ask, "Which verse led you to that conclusion?" or, "What do the rest of you think?"

12. Don't expect every answer to be addressed to you, even though this will probably happen at first. As group members become more at ease, they will begin to truly interact with each other. This is one sign of healthy discussion.

13. Don't be afraid of controversy. It can be stimulating! If you don't resolve an issue completely, don't be frustrated. Move on and keep it in mind for later. A subsequent study may solve the problem.

14. Try to periodically summarize what the group has said about the passage. This helps to draw together the various ideas mentioned and gives continuity to the study. But don't preach.

15. When you come to the application questions at the end of each "Study" section, be willing to keep the discussion going by describing how you have been affected by the study. It's important that we each apply the message of the passage to ourselves in a specific way.

    Depending on the makeup of your group and the length of time you've been together, you may or may not want to discuss the "Respond" section. If not, allow the group to read it and reflect on it silently. Encourage members to make specific commitments and to write them in their study guide. Ask them the following week how they did with their commitments.

16. Conclude your time together with conversational prayer. Ask for God's help in following through on the commitments you've made.

17. End the group discussion on time.

Many more suggestions and helps are found in The Big Book on Small Groups *by Jeffrey Arnold.*

SUGGESTED RESOURCES

Bruce Milne, *Know the Truth: A Handbook of Christian Belief*

J. I. Packer, *Knowing Christianity*

C. Samuel Storms, *The Grandeur of God: A Theological and Devotional Study of the Divine Attributes*

Dallas Willard, *Hearing God: Developing a Conversational Relationship with God*

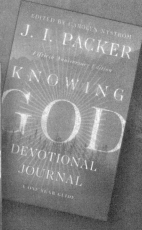